BATTLE

AT

STRAIGHT EDGE

WOODS

BY STEPHEN Shorty MENENDEZ

ISBN-13: 978-1477633885
ISBN-10: 147763388X

BATTLE
AT
STRAIGHT EDGE
WOODS

INTRODUCTION

Vietnam
April 7, 1970

Charlie Company, 3rd Battalion,
22nd Infantry Brigade
25 Infantry Division

This book is not about a single person but of Americans who through the Lottery Draft or volunteered to enlist, bravely served their country from their hearts.

As this story is read you will feel the thoughts and hearts of real men with whom I served. The honesty and commitment they felt to their fellow soldiers is outstanding. Their bravery unheralded. As a unit together we were all great soldiers.

We are all still platoon buddies and have annual reunions to reaffirm our brotherhood to each other. We relive the days of our Vietnam tour at each reunion. We wish we had no memory of the bad days but as soldiers that is our curse.

Nothing good can be said concerning fellow soldiers' deaths. Our sorrow over their death has never and will never be healed. We do remember and love them in memory always.

Importantly we remember our platoon brothers whose lives were sacrificed in the name of freedom. God bless them. I hope I do justice to their memory and our history.

"American Veterans will always be the foundation and beginning of our country's freedom".

"God Bless America"
Author, Stephen 'Shorty' Menendez
'Tunnel Rat At Large'

"Welcome Home to all Combat Veterans"

25th Infantry Division

Combat Infantry Badge

22nd Infantry Brigade

- Preface -

Within this story of a true and heartbreaking battle are letters sent to me from fellow members of Charlie Company, 3rd Battalion, 22nd Infantry Regiment, of the 25th Infantry Division. Their letters recall an unforgettable battle which occurred on April 7, 1970.

I will try my best to insert events that took place during the days prior to the battle. The whole of Charlie Company, 3rd Battalion, 22nd Infantry, of the 25th Infantry Division, fought beyond the call to bravery on that miserable day. Some will never be able to tell of their last day on God's earth. I will try to speak on behalf of our fallen soldiers and friends of this event.

I will describe factual accounts of the battle, including my own recollections and other records written in military Morning Reports. Morning Reports are the military's records of information gleaned from interviewing the unit Commanders and all ground and air units which were called upon to support the men in this battle.

This is our remembrance of a horrible battle fought on April 7, 1970. It's natural that some memory and sequence of events concerning the battle will vary from soldier to soldier over these 40+ years. It's been a painful memory to dredge up but we all felt it should be heard and remembered. A lot of tears were shed while writing these memories.

I pray that those who fell that day rest peacefully in God's hands.

- Contents -

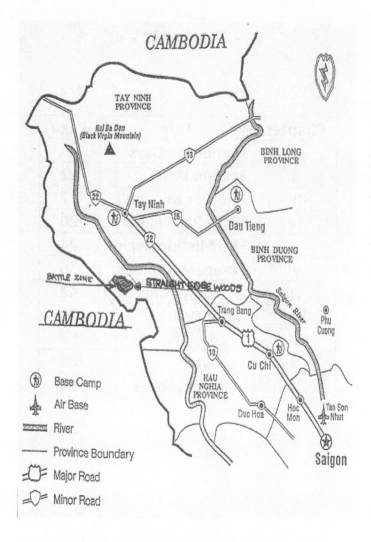

This map shows the Straight Edge Woods. The area marked Battle Zone is where we met the enemy and the battle was fought.

Chapter 1

April 6, 1970
-Numbered Days-

It's another three day ambush mission assigned to the 3rd platoon. We had humped eastward from Fire Support Base Washington in the province of Tay Ninh, Vietnam. Our platoon was operating a 3 day ambush mission not far from Nui Ba Den Mountain. The ominous mountain of Nui Ba Den (Black Virgin Mountain) is a photogenic landmark always in our view. It is also the hiding place for the enemy as they passed troops through this area. The 3200 ft. high mountain of granite boulders is riddled with hollows and natural caves. It is the enemy's safe haven.

Our mission is to intercept the enemy as they made their way through the surrounding jungle to the safety of that mountain. A scheduled three day ambush mission with only one day left until returning back to base camp.

The previous days and nights lying in wait had been quiet for us. Quiet days we often didn't receive. The unbearable heat kept us miserable while waiting for the VC. The entire enemy in Vietnam was technically North and South Vietnamese communists. VC was the slang word for 'Vietnamese Communist '. Most U.S. soldiers called the soldiers from North Vietnam, NVA (North Vietnamese Army). The NVA usually wore a uniform identifying them as North Vietnamese, whereas the local communist sympathizers (VC) wore regular clothing or the infamous 'black pajamas". The local farmers and general public who fought in favor of communism against the southern regimen and the U.S. were referred to as the 'Viet Cong, or VC'. These two references seemed uniform between the different allied forces in South Vietnam. The NVA and VC were all formidable soldiers.

Vietnam's tropical jungle is a natural steam bath from morning until night during this dry season. At night the mosquitos and ground leaches feasted heavily where ever there is exposed skin. Those mosquitos and leaches were stealthier than the enemy.

They always left their bite mark as a calling card. The nights are very long and sleepless. The ground we slept on was always uncomfortable. We never had a good night's sleep in the jungle. At least through this dry season there was no mud to soak through our fatigues. The muggy, damp heat would persist throughout the night to remind us of what the next day would feel like.

I was awakened from a kick to my boot. Gary Stannish said, "Shorty, it's your turn to C-4 the coffee water." After clearing my sleepy eyes and checking for insect bites and leaches, I reached over and shook John Meadows awake. He and Gary Stannish were my close platoon buddies. We regarded each man in our platoon as real brothers. We were all one family sitting in the same dread of war.

Gary Stannish is a tall slim guy from Queens, New York. He, I and Gary Pupshis jointly completed our pre Vietnam training together. We were lucky to be assigned together in the same Infantry unit. It was nice to have someone you knew from the states before going into combat.

John Meadows was a farmer's son from Columbus, Ohio. John and I teamed up together when he arrived in country a few weeks after me.

After scraping away a small patch of dried grass for a cooking fire, I reached into my rut-sack and pinched off a nice nickel size piece of C-4 explosive. C-4 (Composition 4) is a white colored, highly explosive material molded into a brick shape. Some called it plastic explosive. It had the consistency of grainy white clay. We used this stuff primarily for destroying enemy bunkers or tunnels. Word got around that it could be lit with a match and it burned real hot. It could heat a canned C-ration meal or a can of water very fast. It had no lingering smoke or smell to alert any nearby enemy. I heard a rumor that if you stomped on it when it was burning, it would blow your foot off.

The author and Gary Stannish

The Author exiting a tunnel.

I was Charlie Company's 'Tunnel Rat' and proud of it. I could get as much C-4 and TNT as needed for blowing bunkers and tunnels. I had no training on the use of cooking with C-4 before arriving to my unit! I can tell you I never saw or read any evidence that a soldier was injured from cooking with C-4. I will attest from personal experience that it will burn your fingers real fast. The fumes were said to be toxic, but so was breathing most chemicals from the war. Many books have been written on that subject. Many deaths are credited to the military's use of chemicals, then and now.

I used my cleaned C-ration fruit can to heat the coffee water in. The can's lid is bent backwards and then the lid's sides are folded over to make a handle. I lit the nickel size ball of C-4 with a match and then *'insto-presto'*, fire to heat the coffee water.

Heating water with C-4 explosive.

The C–rations instant coffee was dark and bitter. The C-ration breakfast would be, uhh, just C-rations. A delectable, nourishing meal fit only for a tormented starving survivalist. I think we all had our favorite C-ration meal for what little appreciative taste there was. My favorite was the Chicken and Noodles with stale crackers.

Sargent Larry Lowrance, also known as Tennessee, was leading us on this ambush mission. Our originally assigned platoon sergeant, 'SSgt Wayne Brown' was recuperating from a painful and debilitating kidney stone. Many believe the high salt content of the C-rations were partly to blame for the kidney stones.

Sargent Lowrance was a straight forward, no nonsense squad leader. He was well liked and remembered for being the first appointed M-60 Machine Gunner of Charlie Company's Point Squad. He was called Tennessee for the common reason that he came from Bethel, a small town in southwest Tennessee. I liked him because he wasn't much taller than me. I think he was a towering 5 foot 5 inches tall. I actually had to look up to him since I was only 4 foot 10-1/2 inches when I arrived in Vietnam.

We hadn't encountered any enemy so far on this ambush patrol. We were satisfied they were afraid to come around our ambush area. We liked the quiet of our temporary hideaway in the jungle.

It was very hot and humid in Vietnam's jungles. The stifling heat of the day would become only hotter. The enemy was wise and stayed hidden away somewhere; a cooler, shaded place that only they knew about.

Author near Nui Ba Den Mountain

Sgt. Larry Lowrance (L) with his M60
machine gun on his shoulders and Jerry
Kuhns, a platoon member.

Chapter 2
-Second Day-

Steam lifted from the ground as this day's sun rose higher. The humidity and heat pumped the sweat from our bodies. Sweat ran unabated in little streams from head to toe. Our jungle fatigues became stained a darker green color due to the soaking sweat. We almost wished that the night would return and bring relief from this unbearable heat.

It was mid-morning when Sargent Lowrance received a radio message to pack up our squad and get to a PZ (pick up zone) which was about 2 clicks away. (A click = 1000 meters) The orders were passed quietly to each man. We hurriedly packed and secured our equipment as quickly and quietly as possible. We policed the immediate ambush area to afford the enemy nothing we might mistakenly leave behind for his devious use. The VC is very resourceful in using anything to their advantage. A discarded C-ration container can be used to make booby-trap devises or cooking utensils in the same manner as we did. We wanted them to have no advantages. Been there, seen that!

The hump to the PZ was dusty and miserably hot. The sun's heat was blistering. I hated being soaking wet from sweat. The dust lifted from the ground in little clouds as our boots pounded the dried rice fields. It clung to every inch of our exposed skin and sweat dampened clothing. It clung to us like a thin layer of dried plaster. The dust filled our nostrils causing extreme irritation. Our eyes blurred from the burning salty sweat running down from our foreheads.

We reached the PZ location and found a heavy brush area to hide in while waiting for our air lift back to the base camp. We could hardly wait for the sound of the choppers coming to pick us up.

I began thinking of getting back to Fire Support Base Washington and how nice a shower would feel, washing away my caked on layer of dust. Actually it would be a frigid cold shower. I had almost forgotten what a hot shower was like. Almost!

The sound of the approaching choppers thumping rotor blades could be heard long before they came in view. I know we thought about it a hundred times, if we were able to hear the choppers coming so could the enemy. They often tried to pin point the area of the choppers landing to quickly set up an ambush and shoot one or more helicopters down. It would be a horrible sight to behold.

Hot air and acres of dust and dried vegetation swirled around us as the choppers rapidly ascended to pick us up. They came in quick and stopped in a hover just about knee level. We quickly ran and boarded them. The pilot lifted the load of men upwards as soon as the last soldier stepped aboard. This moment of the landing and lift off is the most vulnerable and dangerous time for both the choppers and the men. We can't thank those helicopter crews enough for their risk.

Once the choppers are gaining altitude we began to feel that clean cooler air. There is nothing better than a chopper ride home. The flight back to base camp leaves time to ponder on the ended mission. We felt relief from the heat, dust and fear.

The view from the higher altitude let us appreciate the landscape below. The country was lush with vegetation in most areas.

Some landscape was dead and bleak from chemical spraying. Agent Orange, a deadly defoliant, was heavily used in our area of operations leaving a desolate scarring of the landscape. The altitude also gave us a view, in a military sense, of where we were and where the enemy could be. We took mental notes of streams and paths to later relate them to our land maps.

Ahhh, there's the basecamp coming into our view. That meant just a few more minutes in the air, a quick dusty landing and then it will be *SHOWER TIME*!

John Meadows at Tay Ninh Base Camp.

Chapter 3
-Another Mission-

We walked from the landed choppers toward the base camps entrance. Walking through an opening in multiple rows of razor sharp concertina wire we entered through the camp's gate. We could feel a release of pent up nerves after entering into the security of our base camp. The body tends to relax a little while the mind is still in a tense, *ready* mode. War has a way of keeping the mind that occupied.

Sargent Lowrance told us to clean our weapons and equipment before anyone hit the showers. We did learn to be fast and efficient in gun cleaning, especially after a mission.

The gun cleaning area was constructed from a 55 gallon drum cut in half and affixed to a wooden stand. It was partially filled with diesel fuel to submerse our automatic rifle parts into for cleaning. Showers would follow.

I called dibs on the lowest 155mm Howitzer gun barrel for my shower. My being short has its advantages and disadvantages. The shower was a French style shower bucket holding only about two gallons of water. It was constructed of canvas with a shower head attached to its bottom. You had to go over to the water trailer and fill the bucket. Then you had to ask one of the 155mm Howitzer operators if you could use his barrel end to hang the bucket on. If he wasn't expecting a fire mission he would usually agree. Now you would have to climb up on the track mounted howitzer with the bucket filled with water and walk out to the end of the barrel and hang the bucket off its end. Some of the guys were tall enough to reach the barrels end standing from the ground. Then you walk back down the barrel and off the 155mm howitzer and run to get under the draining bucket. The bucket had an on and off switch so once it is hung you start the water draining. Actually I couldn't have reached the drain switch from the ground. Luckily for me the operator lowered his barrel down for my height. All I have to say about a shower out in the field in Vietnam is, *"it is damn* cold". You do feel wonderful when you are finished and clean.

The supply clerk came around and handed out letters from loved ones back in the real world. John Meadows and I sat at our bunker and shared news written from home. It was nice to hear from home no matter whose family it was from.

It was now past noon as we stood in line for our C-ration lunch. Later for the evening meal the mess Sargent would have a hot meal cooked for us. I never complained about his cooking. It was just the location of his restaurant we didn't enjoy.

While we all sat back and enjoyed our cans of C-rations, Sgt. Lowrance walked up and said, "Lt. Schmidt has a mission meeting for our platoon in ten minutes, eat up".

I'm sure the others almost choked on those words as I did. We couldn't believe it. We just got in and cleaned up and already another mission. It sure pulls the anger out and depresses everyone. We should have known something was up when we got the radio call to come in early from the last mission. *Ah-Heck*, I just thought the First Sargent was missing my companionship.

Chapter 4

-More Bad News-

The platoon gathered at the Sargent's bunker to hear what news Lt. Schmidt had for the new mission. We could see from the Sargent's expression it wasn't going to be good news.

Lt. Schmidt looked at each of us standing in a semi-circle around him. He said, "Men, we have another ambush mission. It's a multi company blocking effort. Our S4 Intelligence group has recent information that a VC resupply unit will attempt to cross from Cambodia into Vietnam in the next few days. It's expected they will come across at or near the Straight Edge Woods. We have had missions near there a few times before so you know the area. Our platoon will leave at 0600 tomorrow morning. Our platoon will be air lifted to an LZ (landing zone) on the east side of Straight Edge Woods. We will check and clear the wood's south edge all the way to the Company's landing area on the west side. We will secure a landing area there for the rest of the company to be air lifted in around 0800 hours the day after our check to the west side. Once our whole company has landed and set up we will wait for the other two companies to join us. It's probably just for a couple days, set up in an ambush blocking force. So get your supplies and then some rest. It will be an early lift off tomorrow morning".

We all waited for the Lieutenant to leave before we began grumbling our dislike of the news. It seemed like we never really obtained any quality rest time. If we weren't pulling an ambush mission or cleaning our equipment someone would be chosen to have the sh*t burning detail.

Could you ever imagine you would be standing all day behind the company's outhouse burning a half of a 55 gallon drum full of sh*t and piss? The purpose is to burn it all so there are no pollution problems.
I never heard of the enemy or even the South Vietnamese soldiers doing this duty.

Your assignment consisted of pulling a heavily used drum of sh*t and piss from under the outhouse seats and pour enough diesel fuel into the mix to hopefully burn it all away. You stand there with a wood or metal pole stirring the putrid mix over and over again until all of it burns away. After it's all burned away the container is shoved back under the outhouse seat and another container is pulled out and you start all over again. Unfortunately for us ours was a five seated outhouse. An all day job rain or shine. I wouldn't wish it on any one again. A toxic duty none of us will ever forget.

Each of us solemnly wandered back to begin collecting the equipment needed for the mission. I was hoping I would be picked for an early or later night guard duty time which afforded more hours of undisturbed sleep. Each man pulled guard duty at night whether at base camp or out in the boonies on a mission.

On the left is Richard Rose and Gary Stannish
is to the right.

A photograph of 3rd Platoon at Tay Ninh Base Camp.

Chapter 5
-The Mission Begins-

The night's stars were still shining brightly as the last person on berm guard duty began waking us. A berm is a dirt wall surrounding a base camp for protection. Trying to find all my equipment in darkness made me feel clumsy even though we had prepared and filled our rut-sacks for the mission the evening before. I always remembered to pack extra instant coffee.

The morning of this mission the mess Sargent had scrambled eggs, toast and coffee ready for us. It was nice not to have C-rations for breakfast. As much as we cherished having a hot meal from the mess hall it would be inevitable that the change of diet from our normal C-rations would cause most of us a bout of diarrhea. We would never mention that to the mess Sargent though. His cooking was good. Better than C-rations.

Our platoon gathered near the camp's gate opening. When Lt. Schmidt arrived he had Sgt. Lowrance take a roll call. Satisfied we were all mission ready, Lt. Schmidt gave the command to leave out of the base camp. The platoon passed through the gate and concertina wires to the PZ. The PZ (pick up zone) was an old dried dirt road which ran from Tay Ninh's main base camp and passed twelve miles north in front of our base, Fire Support Base Washington. The choppers would pick us up on the dirt road.

We didn't have to wait long before the familiar sound of helicopter blades cutting the cooler morning air caught our ears. The men shuffled around gathering in six or eight men groups. In a well-rehearsed movement, the helicopters landed. The platoon quickly boarded the choppers and was ready to go. The pilots pitched the choppers' nose down as they powered their engines to catch forward speed. Like heavy birds they lifted upward and banked away from the base camp. The morning sun was just breaking over the horizon.

The air lift was like a multitude of previous combat flights, bumpy and anxious. No one talked. The cool morning air blowing through the open bodied helicopter was almost cold. We all had our own thoughts about the approaching mission.

The choppers soon began a long sweeping turn. The chopper's pilots would slowly descend before obtaining a direct approach line to the landing area. This was the time our adrenalin increased. We have to anticipate a hot LZ and prepare to take immediate action against any hostile forces. We scanned the upcoming jungle looking for any sight of the enemy.

The pilot forced the chopper downward and brought it to a quick landing approach. The pilots would hold the choppers in a hover two or three feet above the ground allowing a safe distance for us to jump to the ground. Over time we learned to coordinate with the pilots landing methods. We would exit the chopper the instant the pilot banked the choppers nose up and began a hover. It was a cold landing, meaning there was no enemy firing at us. Each man ran from the choppers and placed themselves in a defensive position as the choppers lifted quickly away.

Lt. Schmidt gave hand signals to start the platoon headed in the direction of the jungle.

We were immediately engulfed by the thickness of the jungles entangled growth. Each soldier depended upon all of their experience in jungle warfare to detect anything not friendly. All our senses were stressed to the max with some fear mixed in, hoping we wouldn't have contact with the enemy. Our eyes had to adjust to the steamy darkness caused from the intense thickness of the jungle's canopy. Silvery ribbons of light began to pierce through small openings in the jungle's canopy giving us a hazy view and guiding us through the jungle.

When the last chopper landed with extra supplies we were shocked to see Staff Sargent Brown step off the chopper. He had recovered from his painful kidney stone and has rejoined our platoon.

Each man welcomed him as he made his way to Lt. Schmidt for a quick briefing on the mission. It was a good feeling to have the complete platoon back together again.

3rd Platoon Sargent, SSgt L. Wayne Brown.

As we entered into the jungle, a thin worn path was soon located. It was leading in the same direction we were heading. Gary Pupshis was walking as our platoon point man. He had enough experience and maturity that we trusted in his ability leading the way through the jungle.

Skirting parallel with the path, Gary Pupshis guided the platoon further and deeper into the steamy, thick jungle. I could see the openness of the jungle's edge to our left. It was about 25 meters away. The narrow trail we paralleled was between the field and us.

We humped through the jungle for about 45 minutes when word was passed to take a break in place. The rest break was only long enough for some to drink water from their canteen or have a smoke. Our fatigues were already soaked with sweat.

We started through the jungle again with the platoon now walking on the narrow path nearer to the field's edge. Evidence of enemy sandal marks on the path sharpened our alertness. The platoon had traveled only a few more yards when Gary Pupshis raised his hand in the halt manner. He stood frozen. We strained to see through the jungle trying to see what had alerted him. Gary Pupshis motioned us forward cautiously. He pointed in the direction ahead of himself. Walking a few more steps he halted us again and knelt down. He made a hand motion for SSgt. Brown to come up to his point of view. After a brief discussion, SSgt. Brown signaled the platoon to form in a defensive line behind him. Lt. Schmidt sent John Meadows, Gary Stannish and me, up to assist Gary Pupshis. We inched up quietly next to him. He pointed to a small indented clearing about 5 meters ahead and to the right side of the trail. It was obvious someone had cut away the small bushes edging the trail.

SSgt. Brown squatted next to us and said, "Let's move real cautiously and check that clearing. Meadows, you keep our side towards the field opening covered. Shorty you follow me and Stannish. Keep your eyes open for any movement at all. Let's move".

Gary Pupshis crept forward. His automatic M16 rifle pointed at the clearing ready for any immediate action.

With my eyes checking everywhere, I could not make out any unusual movements in the jungle ahead. Then Gary Pupshis stopped abruptly in his tracks. SSgt. Brown took a couple of quick steps to get close behind him and looked into the small clearing. He slowly turned to me and motioned that I should get up closer with them.

Looking through the dim light into the clearing we could see a back-pack leaned against the taller grass at the clearing's far side. We stepped cautiously searching up to the clearing. We studied every inch of the small cleared opening for the enemy or possible booby traps. Our nerves were on edge. Gary Pupshis motioned to us that he was going to check the back pack. SSgt. Brown nodded his approval along with a hand and facial expression to be very careful.

Gary Pupshis laid his rifle on the ground but still within his reach. With his left hand braced on the ground he leaned over the backpack to study its back side area. Giving a thumbs up signal he began running his fingers around the bottom edge of the pack. Each touch feeling for a wire or anything remotely suggesting it was booby trapped. With sweat glistening on the back of his neck, Gary Pupshis sat upright to relax the ache in his back. He wiped sweat from his brow with his left forearm. The air was humid and heavy making it hard to breathe under this kind of intense pressure. Gary turned the back-pack around revealing three anti-tank rounds, known as RPG's (rocket propelled grenades) attached to it.

The other members of the platoon kept their vigilance of security until we gave them the "all clear" signal. Relief showed on each face of the platoon members when the all clear signal was motioned to them.

Not wanting to expose our position we decided to leave the clearing as we found it. Gary Pupshis replaced the pack exactly in the same position it had laid. If we had decided to blow up the back-pack of RPG rounds, our location would have been known to the enemy for miles around.

Lt. Schmidt signaled the platoon to move forward and we continued to clear the west side of the jungle.

The Lieutenant signaled for the platoon to stop late in the afternoon. We would set up for the night and continue the last 50 yards to the landing field in the morning.

Shorty (author) waiting for a chopper ride.

SSgt. Sargent L. Wayne Brown waiting in the jungle. Notice the field phone handset hanging from the tree.

Chapter 6
July 7, 1970
- The Company Landing-

The platoon left the damp humid jungle on its west side. The bright morning sun was already blinding and hot. One by one we left the jungle and crossed into a dried rice patty. Lt. Schmidt directed the platoon to set up along an old berm line about 75 - 100 feet away from the wood line. We sat in the dried rice patty field, which was long ago abandoned by local villagers. Their fields now only sun dried grass and thick dust. The berms which once held water for rice crops had weathered over time to half their normal height, only reaching 12 to 14 inches high. The berms gave us something to rest against while waiting for the landing of additional Charlie Company troops.

We sat facing the expanse of jungle called the Straight Edge Woods. To our west were open fields of old rice farming plots. At our south was a line of brush and immature trees. It ran west from the wood's edge to the far open fields towards Cambodia.

To our north about 75 feet away was a large termite mound with a small leafless tree growing from its center. The rice patty berm we rested against connected at the termite mound and then turned 90 degrees back towards the wood line. There was nothing else out there except clear blue skies and a burning hot sun. The wood's edge was very long and almost 'straight edged'.

With only time for us to drink some water, the choppers carrying our Company could be heard on their approach. We welcomed the strength of a full Company of our friends joining us.

In a single file of eight helicopters the first of our Company began landing. Soldiers with heavily laden field packs quickly jumped from the choppers and regrouped at the nearest berm location.

A second group of choppers followed and landed their eager cargo of soldiers. This continued until the whole Company had been landed.

The Mortar Platoon had landed and was quickly deployed to an old bomb crater next to the wood line. This position was good for the close artillery support which the mortar team could provide us. They set up quickly while the company was being organized into proposed defensive positions.

The area was getting crowded with our company of men so Lt. Schmidt had us move down the berm line away from the termite mound. The termite mound was taken over as a place for the Company Commander's position. Away from the Company Commanders position we spread ourselves about a yard apart with Lt. Schmidt and his radio man in the center of our platoon's line. It was getting real hot waiting in the sun.

John Meadows sat next to me with Gary Stannish in line north of me along the berm. Dale Erdman was next in line to my south with Phillip Martin and Bob (Doc) Brault, our medic. We awaited orders to move into the woods and set up an ambush position.

Time seemed to drag on waiting in the hot sun. Phillip Martin stated he couldn't wait any longer. He needed to relieve himself urgently. He let us all know he was headed to the woods to take a dump. He then disappeared into the wood line, into that maze of thick brush and trees.

We waited for the lieutenant to give orders for us to move into the woods and set up for the ambush. Suddenly, *crack, bam! Crack crack, bam*! Rifle shots rang out from inside the wood line. We could tell it was an AK47 and an M16 in the exchange. Everyone was momentarily stunned and jumped behind the berm line. Lt. Schmidt yelled. "Who's missing, who's in the woods?" We jointly yelled that it was Phillip Martin in the woods. Lieutenant Schmidt quickly conferred with the captain on the situation. Lt. Schmidt and his radio man, Gary Stannish, headed to the wood line and yelled for Martin. A couple seconds had lapsed when Martin yelled, "I'm coming out, don't shoot, don't shoot." Immediately Martin sprang from the heavy woods in a full out run yelling, *"Gooks in the woods, gooks in the woods"*. The name Gook' is a slang reference to a VC or an NVA soldier. He didn't stop until he jumped behind the berm line between me and J.D. Meadows. The lieutenant came over the berm and asked Martin what had occurred. Martin said, "I was looking for a place to go to the bathroom when all of a sudden two gooks with AK'S (automatic Russian rifle) came down a little trail in my direction. They were about 40 feet from me when we saw each other. I dove towards a low spot beside the trail. The gooks opened up on me and I returned fire. The gooks fired back a second time then fled further back into the woods. That's when I heard you call my name. Damn', they nearly got me!"

The Lt. radioed to the Captain relaying the enemy contact information. The Captain ordered the Company to take full defensive positions along the berm line facing the woods.

We noticed Martin had a mark just below his left eyebrow. It was raw flesh, like a burn mark. "What is that?" I asked pointing to his left eyebrow. Martin felt the injured spot and exclaimed,"*DAMN*, I was grazed by the gooks AK47 round." He rubbed the spot and grimaced at the pain. The wound was about 1-1/2 inches long. Definitely an enemy's bullet had grazed his lower eye brow. He was Lucky, lucky, lucky!

Our concentration was heavily focused on the wood line. Word was passed to keep low and observe the woods for any movement. Our focus was intense when an acrid, rotten aromatic smell broke our concentration simultaneously along the berm line. It became obvious that the heavy smell of piss and excrement was emanating from Martin. I now understood what the statement," having the pee and poop scared out of you", meant. For a brief moment I wondered if this had happened to Martin in the woods. I know it would have been enough for me to relieve myself unconsciously.

"Martin, what's that smell on you" we asked? Martin had a weird look on his face and said, "I guess those gooks were headed for their shitter when I jumped into it for cover when they began shooting at me. I hadn't noticed it until now. "

Martin sure smelled *bad*. We couldn't tease him too much at that moment, considering the circumstances. But it was *BAAAD!*

Chapter 7
- A Deadly Time-

The Captain was busy organizing the Company's position. Everyone had readied themselves for imminent contact. The heat from the sun definitely was not on our side. The hype of our nerves and the tormenting heat became exhausting. Our helmets felt like an oven on high heat. Water was being consumed heavily. The word was passed to conserve our water for now.

It didn't take much to know the enemy would be organizing just like us. Their advantage was they had the security of being in the woods. We had no idea of their strength in numbers or how well armed they may be. We were soon to find all that out.

Suddenly automatic rifle fire erupted from the wood line. The berm spit dirt into the air directly in front of us. We were pinned down and trying to get closer to the ground than ever before. Every time we rose up to fire back, the berm exploded from the enemy gun fire. *We were trapped*!

Heavy enemy machinegun fire continued to erupt all along the wood line. Explosions from RPG rockets hit in the area of the Mortar Squad. The mortar squad was immediately disabled by the enemy. Everyone was now involved in contact with the enemy. We returned fire at the enemy and they returned fire back just as heavy. It was quickly becoming apparent they had us pinned down and we couldn't change our position in any direction. As word traveled through the company that we had lost the lives of men in the other platoons, we all realized the enemy gun fire was deadly accurate. I couldn't believe how fast this was all happening.

Looking to our south we noticed a couple figures running towards the woods. They didn't resemble our men in jungle fatigues but looked rather suspiciously like VC. This was reported to our Captain by Lt. Schmidt. The Captain ordered us not to fire on them because he was expecting another Company from that direction to connect with us. They sure didn't *look* like our guys.

We were all busy reloading magazines and getting grenades ready as SSgt. Brown checked on his men's readiness in the third platoon. We were glad to have him back with us. The automatic rifle fire was still being heavily exchanged.

We heard from SSgt. Brown that we couldn't expect any artillery support. All available artillery units were supporting other units in heavy enemy contact. This sure made us feel rather insignificant under the circumstances. Without our mortar squad we had no close artillery support. This was becoming a *"kiss your ass goodbye"* situation.

Lt. Schmidt had the Platoon Sergeants going up and down the line providing information. It was told that the Captain had ordered an "on line assault" against the wood line, commencing within moments. I couldn't believe my ears. I thought, "Assault against a wood line of a hidden enemy"? We couldn't even estimate the enemy's size. Their strength of numbers was totally unknown and they had us dead to rights.

"Online everyone, NOW!" the order was given by Lt. Schmidt. We obeyed the given order. We stepped forward towards the wood line firing into the trees and brush. The continuous automatic rifle fire was deafening. A grenade round from John Meadows firing his M79 Grenade launcher exploded at the edge of the wood line. It caused a momentary pause in the automatic enemy gun fire, but it was only momentary. I didn't see any enemy but I heard their rounds whistling past my head and body. I was numb with fear and anxiety. Why were we doing this assault?

I had Gary Stannish standing at my left shoulder and Dale Erdman to my right as we progressed toward the wood line. John Meadows was a step or two behind firing his M79 grenade launcher into the wood line. He was very accurate with the M79.

We took one more step forward when I heard Dale Erdman make an unusual guttural sound. I looked to my right to see Dale with his chin pressed tightly to his chest. Blood was gushing freely covering the front of his chest. His hand went to his throat. I thought, *"My God! Dale is hit"*. He fell to the ground mortally wounded. Immediately our medic, Doc (Bob Brault) was at his side. We kept firing at the wood line with intense revenge in mind.

"*Cease fire! Cease fire!*" Lt. Schmidt shouted, "Return to the berm line". The order was shouted over and over. It was a great relief. We *didn't* waste any steps getting back to the berm. The enemy was still firing heavily when I jumped to get over the berm. I looked back towards the wood line when I heard SSgt. Brown yell out, "someone go and help Meadows". While his words echoed in my ears I saw John Meadows laying on the ground only a few yards away looking over at me. Time seemed to stop. It seemed surreal seeing my friend laying there. I reared up to get over the berm to help him when the enemy opened up with automatic machine gun fire. The berm in front of our position burst apart with enemy rounds. It was evident the enemy was using Meadows as bait. I was pinned down and prevented from helping my friend. I felt helpless. At that moment Gary Stannish made a great giant step over the berm and pulled Meadows to safety. Gary made a *heroic* rescue saving John Meadows from certain death.

John Meadows was wounded badly in his hip. He now lay on his side behind the safety of the berm waiting for a medic to help him. His hip was a mass of blood and dirt. He still had the camaraderie to give me a "thumbs up" sign.

The enemy was changing their tactics. Enemy snipers had been positioned along the wood line attempting to target and kill anyone visible in their sights. Trying to retrieve our killed was impossible.

We still had no artillery support. A medevac helicopter was reportedly on its way to evacuate our dead and wounded. We would have to use heavy suppressive weapons fire against the wood line to enable the medevac helicopter to safely land. There was no time to think. We just did what needed to get done.

We could hear the medevac helicopter in the distance. It was approaching from our rear. We turned and saw the helicopter coming closer and closer. Our Company began firing at the wood line with a heavy volley of suppressive gun fire. The medevac chopper was coming straight at our position when in an instant of shock and disbelief, the helicopter was hit with machine gun fire across its' front canopy. The helicopter immediately rolled to its side and abruptly crashed just several feet behind us.

The sound of the helicopter hitting the ground was horrendous. Men were yelling in fear. I can't describe it in words. It was just terrible. Everyone was momentarily stunned.

SSgt. Brown and the rest of us disregarded the enemy and the battle that was raging and ran to the helicopter. We found one crew member had been tossed out when it hit the ground. The pilot was fatally wounded. The co-pilot was wounded in both his lower legs. He couldn't get loose from his seat harness because he couldn't use his legs to brace himself. He was jammed forward in his seat. The door gunner had a broken arm. The medic crew member was uninjured and helped with the removal of his fellow crew.

While we helped cut the injured co-pilot free from his harness belts we noticed the helicopter was now burning. The co-pilot said there was a whole case of M79 grenade rounds in the cockpit. The M79 grenades and the M60 machineguns with ammunition were hurriedly removed. If they had exploded we would have lost many men along the berm line.

The enemy's automatic gun fire gained in its intensity. The men along the berm close to the burning chopper crawled away from the intense flames. The crew members were carried and dragged to a safe area away from the burning coffin which still held their brave but fatally wounded pilot.

All attempts had failed to free the fatally wounded pilot. The canopy was crushed preventing his rescue. We cried silently as we watched the helicopter burn. It only took minutes for it to melt down to a gray pile of melted metal. Only the tail section and parts of the blades were still recognizable. A real 'Hero' had died trying to rescue our fellow fallen soldiers.

Our 3rd Platoon Medic, (Doc.) Bob Brault.

All our medics had to deal with the injuries and death which incurred in battle that day. Many men survived because of their heroic efforts in combat conditions.

To all our medics, 'Thank you'.

Chapter 8
-More Hell-

The relentless scorching sun had exhausted our water supply. Resupply was called for and should be arriving soon. My skin felt like charred leather. Our eyes were blood-shot from the sweat and gun smoke in our eyes. Contact with the enemy had only been about an hour in time but seemed like an eternity.

The enemy showed they wanted us dead. The battle continued with us still pinned down behind an ever diminishing berm line. I swear it shrunk a couple inches each time we were fired upon.

SSgt. Brown passed the word that air support was on its way. He said we should hug the ground real close because jets would be dropping their bombs "deadly close". The woods, only 100 ft. away, was closer than deadly close for me.

The first F105 Thunder Chief jets gave no warning to their approach. The F105 jets came screaming across the tree tops as one by one their bombs began falling. When the bombs exploded, it hurt. The concussion hit us hard. The ground shuddered lifting a cloud of dust all around us. I know it didn't do the enemy any good either. The F105 jets also made several passes with Napalm (a jellied gas bomb which when exploded, the flames stuck and burned everything). I saw the load of Napalm canisters twirling through the air heading directly to the location of the enemy. I got even closer to the ground for protection before it hit. I could feel the ground again shudder when they struck. Thick black smoke billowed towards the sky followed by swirls of massive burning flames. The air tasted of diesel fuel as the black smoke drifted over us. It was a fiery, deadly hell for many of the enemy.

Following the F105 jets was a squadron of A1 Sky Raiders flying in a tight formation looking like a surreal old time WWII movie. These planes were able to stay in contact much longer than a F105 jet. Their gas engines needed much less fuel to burn. Each plane made a strafing pass with their 20mm cannons directed at the enemy positions. The A1s circled around and would begin another strafing pass.

Their propeller engines whined to a faster and higher pitch as they dove and dropped 250 lb. bombs on the enemy. It was a fantastic sight. They sure did an amazing job of protecting us.

We lay behind the berm waiting to see if the enemy's fighting spirit had been extinguished. During this ground shaking bombardment the medics were meticulously attending to the severely wounded men.

Lt. Schmidt had reported to the Captain regarding our wounded and killed and the safety of the remaining helicopter crew. Lieutenant Schmidt returned back to our position and was talking to SSgt. Brown about where another rescue helicopter would land, when an enemy's shot rang out. The Lieutenant fell to the ground yelling loudly, clutching his left knee. A sniper had shot him directly in his left knee cap. The exiting bullet left a ragged hole at the back of his calf. He was in terrific pain. Who would get shot next?

SSgt. Brown was now our platoon leader. Lt. Schmidt was being bandaged by Doc. Brault as he lay behind the berm in horrible pain. It was evident with our killed and wounded that another medevac was now severely needed.

John Meadows was in terrible pain and couldn't be moved easily. All our wounded and killed would need to be hand carried to a medevac when it arrived. The heat and stress of battle was compounding the pain to our wounded. Our minimal water supply was passed to them to help appease the heat. I was sure hoping this would all end soon.

In the distance we could hear the sound of the rotors of another helicopter. A Cobra gunship circled above our rice paddy field to our rear. A second chopper was also coming into view at a lower altitude and headed straight towards us. The second chopper was another medevac chopper and this time was landing to our rear about 300 to 400 feet.

SSgt. Brown yelled over to Gary Stannish to get ready to evacuate John Meadows. We could see others had already headed toward the medevac carrying our KIA's (Killed in Action) and other wounded soldiers. It was difficult to watch this happening only yards away. The enemy increased its firing trying to kill the soldiers carrying our KIA'S and wounded to the medevac chopper. The enemy weapon fire was intense. It would be a tragedy if the medevac chopper with our wounded and dead was shot down.

SSgt. Brown yelled over to Gary Stannish to start heading to the medevac with John Meadows.

John grunted heavily with stifling pain as Gary lifted and supported him. Blood covered John's hip and leg area. I almost broke down, seeing my friend in that condition.

Gary held most of John's weight as they both hobbled toward the medevac chopper. The enemy began firing at Gary and John as they crossed the barren killing field. They would have to endure a hellish slow walk before reaching the medevac chopper.

Then SSgt. Brown yelled out, "Shorty, grab ahold of the lieutenant's trouser legs and help me carry him to the chopper".

I jumped up and grabbed the lieutenant's pants legs. SSgt. Brown had grasped the lieutenant's shoulder harness as we lifted him.

The lieutenant's knee was bent toward me. The bandage had slipped down from his knee and exposed the hole made from the enemy's bullet. I starred at the bullet's hole in amazement and sorrow. I heard the Lieutenant moan as we lifted him from the dried, blood soaked earth were he lay. SSgt. Brown and I began carrying him across the open field. The medevac chopper seemed to be farther away as we were trying to carry the Lieutenant without dropping him. Even though he only weighed about 160 pounds, the Lieutenants weight seemed to increase with each step. I wasn't sure if I could hold onto him all the way across the field to the medevac chopper.

My shoulders ached from the lieutenant's weight, but I was proud to be with SSgt. Brown helping to carry our lieutenant to the waiting medevac chopper.

I was exhausted and thought we would be safe the closer we got to the chopper. I was wrong. Within a few steps of getting the Lt. on the chopper we could hear the enemy's bullets hitting the sides of the medevac chopper's hull. Enemy bullets whizzed past us. We were definitely a target in the enemy's sights.

We lifted the Lieutenant with all our strength laying him onto the chopper floor. I looked over and saw John Meadows lying there looking at me. His terrible pain showed on his face. I also saw the poncho covered bodies of our other friends. I was standing there in a daze of exhaustion when SSgt. Brown hit me on the shoulder and yelled, "Let's get back to the berm; they're trying to kill us out here in this open field".

The medevac chopper lifted away in a swirl of dust and dried grass as we ran back towards the berm. I just couldn't believe all this was happening.

As I got behind the berm I looked back towards the fading medevac chopper and wondered if John, the Lieutenant and the others would be ok, and would I ever see them again.

Chapter 9
-Regrouping-

The last available air support had exhausted their fire power and were returning to their base. The persistent enemy snipers still kept us pinned behind the berm. It was evident that we couldn't keep our position without more men being killed or wounded.

Most of the company's men had depleted their water. Between the sun and our ragged nerves we were feeling weak and miserable. The musty dust scratched at our dry mouth and throats. Our fatigues had long lines of dried, white salt from our drying perspiration. This must be *HELL*.

SSgt. Brown came along the berm and told each man to get ready to pull back further away out into the field. We would crawl away until we were about 300 yards from the wood line and wait for the whole Company to join us and form a protective perimeter. We would make our stand waiting in the open field under the sun's blistering heat.

The crawl was back breaking under the hot sun and we needed the water resupply soon. The rest of the company was moving in platoon size groups into the open dry field. Each platoon was assigned an area forming a company sized perimeter. What would the enemy decide to do next?

The word was passed along to dig in and be ready for a counter attack. Only a few of us had shovels with which to dig. We weren't expecting the mission to be in an open unprotected field. We used our helmets, knives and bare hands to scratch a minimal depression of protection from the surface of the dried field. We were grateful just to take a moments rest away from the enemy.

The day passed into twilight as we waited for the enemy. I hoped they had had enough fighting and would just go away. We prepared for a long nights stay.

The night's darkness fell upon us bringing new feelings of fear and uncertainty. We would have little warning if the enemy decided to leave their safety of the jungle and attack us while they were cloaked in darkness. I believe none of the men in our Company rested that night.

We were alerted at about midnight that enemy movement was detected at the wood's edge. Each platoon's Sargent was equipped with a night starlight scope. The scope could see into the darkness using the stars and moon's light to enhance objects. It was evident the enemy was amassing in large numbers. Would they attack us?

All the men prepared themselves for a second battle. We knew we were outnumbered heavily. Bayonets were affixed to our rifles. I couldn't hear a sound except the thump of my heart in my ears. We all stared at the wood line trying to pin point the enemy but the darkness had hidden them. Time lingered in anticipation and fear.

"They're leaving". The word was quickly passed from man to man. The enemy had gathered at the wood's edge and began to proceed back towards the Cambodian border. Nervous fear was replaced by exhausted relief like an ocean's wave throughout the company of men. The night was now dead quiet and cool. I rolled onto my back and stared at the stars. I remember

feeling shaky, not knowing if it was from the toll of the battle and heat or from the night's coolness.

The darkness seemed endless as we each took turns on night watch. It wasn't absolute that the enemy had departed permanently. We waited.

Chapter 10
- Relieved-

It was a joy to see the haze of a new day's sun rise beginning to appear. We all stared at the wood line not knowing what to expect. I knew we would return for our killed brothers which we were unable to retrieve during the battle. I knew we would cry.

We waited for Bravo Company to approach around the northwest side of the woods before we crossed the field back to our embattled berm. The woods still smoked from the previous day's fighting and air attack. When we reached the berm I walked to where the medevac chopper had crashed and burned. There wasn't much left of the helicopter, just pieces of the main rotor blades and the tail section. There was no sign of the entombed pilot.

I could see where John Meadows had rested next to the berm and spilled his blood on the ground. The leg of his blood stained jungle fatigue trousers still lying where Doc. Brault had cut it away from his wounded hip. I missed my friend. I hoped him well.

The members of Charlie Company over looked the battle grounds with a blank stare. We were completely exhausted, mind and body.

We were told an airlift was inbound to pick us up and return us to Tay Ninh Base Camp. We only had moments to regroup before the choppers were descending to lift us away from this place.

Bravo Company would stay to sweep through the woods and be witness to the battles death and destruction. They would endure the mournful retrieval of our dead. I was glad to leave this place.

It wouldn't be until our return to base camp that we would hear the extent of our casualties. There wasn't much conversation once we landed. We all went to our bunkers and looked for solace from our experience.

How does one really explain their feelings after a battle? These are feelings which will haunt us for our life time.

Chapter 11
-Soldier's Letters-

SP/4 Gary Stannish
Nick name – *Stan the Man* & *New York*
3rd Platoon (THIRD HERD)
11B Rifleman, Radio man
Home Town: Queens, N.Y

On the morning of April 7, 1970, our platoon was flown by chopper to the Straight Edge Woods. We were dropped off about 50 yards from the wood line. We quickly set up behind a rice paddy dike that gave us protection. Capt. Pride set up behind a very large dirt mound.

The weather was clear and hot with the only available shade being in the woods. A little time had passed when automatic rifle fire came from the woods. We all dove behind the rice paddy dike and did a quick name check to see if anyone from our platoon was missing. Pvt. Phillip Martin was missing. Capt. Pride told LT. Schmidt to take me with a radio and go get Martin.

We started to the woods in a run until we were about 20 feet from its edge then we crawled the final 20 feet. At the woods edge we called out to Martin who quickly answered. Martin was about 30-40 feet inside the woods and so were the enemy. The LT. and I fired toward the enemy giving Martin time to run to us. With Martin safely with us I radioed to the Captain to hold fire while we ran from the woods.

I remember the Captain ordering the whole company to commence an online assault towards the wood line. I remember Dale Erdman was shot in the neck and died.

Later during the contact with the enemy John Meadows was shot in the hip. I stepped over the dike and pulled him safely behind it. I remember LT. E. Schmidt was shot in the knee. He was in pain but still managed to hand me his camera to take a photo of his wounded knee. I saw Shorty Menendez and SSgt. Brown carrying him to the medevac chopper.

Capt. Pride wanted us to do another assault but I believe we all refused. I'm not sure of that refusal though. I remember we later moved away from the woods and set up a night position.

I think the leadership of Capt. Pride sucked. He should have been court martialed.

~~~~~~~~

SP/4 Charles Zimmer
11b Rifleman, Radio man
Home Town: Port Huron, Michigan

Hi Shorty, it's been a long time.

I remember you were the Company's Tunnel Rat. I will try to tell what I remember of that day.

Captain Lawson R. Pride was the Company Commander of Charlie Company. On April 7, 1970 the company was supposed to dig in at the wood line of Straight Edge Woods to conduct an ambush on the enemy.

The South Vietnamese soldiers were supposed to go into Cambodia and flush out the enemy towards our ambush sight. We were told it may take a couple of days before the enemy would reach our position.

We were air lifted by Huey helicopters to a field near the wood line. The Company was getting ready to move closer towards the woods when suddenly the crack of AK 47's (enemy automatic rifle) was heard. After a few moments the enemy was ripping us apart with their automatic rifle fire. We were caught in the open field. Our company of men was scrambling to find cover. There were a few bomb craters if you were lucky to dive into one. Other than that there was just that shallow berm line from an old, dried up rice paddy.

The enemy was already in the woods and dug in well. The point man on our right flank was hit by enemy fire. His platoon Sergeant went to get him, he also was killed. Their Lieutenant tried to help them and he died alongside his men.

The men died in about a half hour period of time. No one could help them. The enemy snipers killed anyone who attempted a rescue.

The Company commander called over my radio that he was pinned down. He had me direct all the incoming bombs, napalm and 30mm cannon near his position.

We were lucky to be in one of the few bomb craters directing the jet's bombing and 30mm cannons. The sound was deafening at times. The enemy fired RPG's (anti-tank weapons) at our position which wounded several men. Our mortar platoon which was closest to the wood line was immediately destroyed.

The fighting continued all day. Late in the afternoon the Captain ordered a pull back several hundred yards away from the wood line.

The Captain radioed in for resupplies and a ground radar unit. The radar unit would detect movement at night. We settled into a perimeter and waited as the darkness fell.

About midnight the portable radar detected movement at the wood line. The movement continued for about a half hour. We all waited for a night attack against our position. The man controlling the radar said the movement was heading along the wood line away from us. We sure were glad they left the area.

The next morning we all returned to the woods to recover our fallen soldiers. That's all I have to say. Thanks for this opportunity to reconcile with my brothers of Charlie Company.

<center>~~~~~~~~</center>

Bobby Joliff
2nd. Platoon
11B, Rifleman – Co. Radioman
Home Town: West Plains, Missouri

Viet Nam April 7, 1970

The third platoon was going around the south side of Straight Edge Woods on recon and to secure the LZ for the rest of the company. I was the Company radio operator for the Command Post in 2nd. Platoon. Bruce

Mills was the Battalion radio man. We had been in the field on a search and destroy mission when we were called upon to meet up with the 3rd platoon at Straight Edge Woods.

We were picked up on April 7th, 1970 about 0730 hours. The flight wasn't very long before we were dropped off in a dried out rice field. On the landing approach I saw our Company Mortar Squad setting up in a bomb crater next to the wood line. After several air-lifts the whole company was in the field. We waited for 3rd platoon to come around the wood line and join us. Bruce and I sat down next to a small tree and removed our back packs containing our radios.

From my and Bruce's position we didn't know what started the battle, but the jungle exploded with enemy fire. Bruce and I picked the wrong tree in the wood line to rest next to because when it all started we were across a small rice paddy from the rest of the company. We immediately got on our radios which already was full of chatter. The company commander was calling in an air strike and pleading for artillery support. Bruce and I decided to run for it to the company's safety of an old rice paddy dike. It looked like the company was a hundred yards away. The enemy was firing everywhere around us. At that time I became scared.

I remember calling out on the radio for a dust-off medevac for casualties.

I was already feeling the heat and reached for my canteen when I noticed my leg was wet. My first thought was that I was wounded but I felt no pain. My canteen had been hit by the enemy's bullet, now that's luck.

I felt helpless as the medevac chopper was shot down killing the pilot. The crashed chopper was very close to 3rd platoon and was burning.

The enemy continued fighting us all day. I was sure grateful when the fighting stopped.

The next morning we returned to our base camp and mourned for our buddies killed and wounded.

All the battles our group endured seemed to run together one after another in my mind. All the men of Charlie Company were a hell of a great team. I'll never forget the sounds of that battle. I can still hear the Jets dropping their bombs and napalm on the enemy. I feel the continuous fury of the M60 machine guns and all the men returning fire to the enemy, and the heavy smoke making the air hard to breath.

We really pounded those little bastards but they still continued fighting us. They lost a lot of men that day.

Shorty, it seems like there are a lot of other things to say about that day but I can't find the words right now. I'll see you soon.

Bobby Joliff

~~~~~~~~

Captain M.C. TOYER
Company Commander, Bravo Company
October 1969- August 1970
Home Town: Pilot Point, Texas

I was the Company Commander for Bravo Company and our Company also participated in this operation on April 7th, 1970 called "Task Force King". I do not remember which other units may have been involved on this day. "Task Force King's" mission was essentially as a blocking force while a mechanized unit was to sweep toward Charlie Company's position.

I recall a Ranger (75TH Rangers unit) patrol had a significant contact in the same vicinity just a few days prior to this mission. There is a detailed report online from the 25th Division IDA web site.

Bravo Company had spent the night (April 6th) before at Fire Support Base Washington, and then was flown the next morning to the same woods vicinity near Charlie Company. It was supposed to be a one day mission.

We encountered fresh trails and tunnels. We suffered two soldiers wounded from booby traps.

Bravo Company set up about 1 klick (1000 meter measurement on a grid map) from Charlie Company on the opposite side of the same woods. I was not comfortable with our location with the only protection being a low rice paddy dike. We were about 200 meters from the wood line.

As soon as my second lift of men had landed, Lt. Candela and his second platoon made a searching sweep of the woods to our front but found no recent activity. The night of April 6th was uneventful.

I continued to send out small patrols and reinforced our position as much as possible. We had no overhead cover so we used poncho liners.

I was aware of Charlie Company's position but our patrols never linked up with each other. We never had visual contact either. When Charlie Company made contact with the enemy on April 7th we had live fire over our position but couldn't be sure if it came from Charlie Company or the enemy in the woods. I believe the enemy nearest to us was only a small unit acting as a rear guard.

I don't recall any artillery support or gunship support, probably because of the close proximity to our two companies and the Mechanized unit. We could have provided mortar support for Charlie Company but never received a fire mission. I guess Charlie Company and the enemy were just too close together in combat.

Early the next morning we went to the battle area of Charlie Company to complete a sweep of the enemy's position. Charlie Company was picked up and flown back to the base camp. I specifically recall the downed medevac helicopter. We found enemy documents, equipment and heavy blood trails in the wood line. The enemy had removed their comrade's bodies during the night. The documents revealed later the enemy was part of an NVA Regiment.

Just after this operation Lt. Candela was transferred to Charlie Company to replace Lt. Hill who died from the wounds he received on that mission.

All of our soldiers fought bravely on this combined mission.

I hope to see you at the next reunion Shorty.

M.C. TOYER

Eric C. Schmidt
Nick name – L.T.
1st Lieutenant, 3rd Platoon Leader
Charlie Company, 3/22nd
25th. Infantry Division
February 1970 – April 1970

Straight Edge Woods, April 7, 1970

Charlie Company had been on a company size operation for a couple of days when we were informed that we would be picked up and inserted into a new location. I believe we were three platoons along with the mortar platoon (4th platoon) would be air lifted to our position. We began this mission on April 7th, 1970 being air lifted to a wood lined field. It was a hot, dry and dusty day.

I recall arriving and noticing that Lt. Hill's platoon was grouped up making the landing area crowded and unsafe. Not wanting my platoon so exposed and grouped up I moved them away from the rest of the company further along a paddy dike parallel to the wood line. It was only a short period of time while troops and supplies were arriving that one of my men (Phillip Martin) decided to go in the wood line to take a leak. It seemed men in the first platoon had done the same.

Now the sh*t hit the fan. Small arms fire popped off for about five rounds. Then my men yelled that Phillip Martin was inside the wood line. I took my radio man with me to the wood line to find my missing man. We made contact with him at the edge of the woods as the firing momentarily halted. Martin, me and my radioman ran back to the rice paddy dike. As we reached the berm, automatic gun fire erupted all along the wood line. Everyone began returning fire in the direction of the wood line. I couldn't see the events occurring in the other platoons positions but the radio was calling out that somewhere along the line we had wounded soldiers. I was busy making sure my men were doing their best and kept safe. Every time we moved the berm exploded from enemy fire. I was frustrated not knowing how many enemy we were facing. They had the advantage of concealment inside the wood line; we were fully exposed with only that low berm to lie behind.

I received orders from the Captain that 2nd and 3rd platoon would advance online firing at the wood line to overpower the enemy. He and first platoon would advance also. I and my men left the safety of the berm line at the Captain's command. I had my M60 machine gunners lay low and supply suppressive fire continuously. We were immediately met with very heavy enemy fire. Some of the men knelt low to fire and tried to avoid being hit by the enemy. This assault seemed to go bad rather quickly. We were now pinned down and could advance no further. At this time I was informed that Dale Erdman had been hit. Our medic, 'Robert Brault' had quickly begun attending to him. It was a necessity that we crawl back to the berm to avoid being a continuous open target for the well dug in enemy. I gave the order to return to the berm. It was a difficult crawl back, that distance to the berm.

When we reached the berm I saw John Meadows still a few yards away calling for help. He was wounded and couldn't move. I yelled for someone to get him. I saw Shorty

Menendez make an attempt but machine gun fire pinned him down. Gary Stannish jumped up and with only two long strides had grabbed John Meadows and pulled him over the berm. I was lucky more of my men weren't injured or killed.

I heard over the radio that we had wounded and KIA's in the other platoons also.

After conferring with SSgt. Brown I low-crawled to the Captains position to arrange a medevac for the wounded. An area approximately 25 meters behind 3rd platoon was picked to pick up the wounded.

We were still receiving heavy enemy fire when I was radioed that the medevac chopper was coming in. I could see the chopper coming from our rear at about six to ten feet above the ground. The pilot nearing our position began his hover and instantly began taking heavy enemy fire. Before the pilot could pull the chopper away the helicopter's canopy was riddled with machine gun fire, killing him. The chopper reeled over sideways and strut the ground hard. The rotors thrashed at the ground wildly, breaking into pieces and were thrown in every direction. Before the rotors quit turning, the chopper began burning. I and several of my men ran to the chopper to assist in removing the crew.

The crew members had been wounded. The co-pilot had wounds to both his legs and it was hard to extract him. The door gunner had arm injuries but was shouting that there was a whole case of M79 Grenade ammunition in the chopper. If that ammunition would explode with the crashed helicopter only a few feet from my men there would be untold casualties. We located and removed the M79 grenades from the chopper along with two M60 machine guns and their ammunition. The chopper was now fiercely burning preventing us from removing the killed pilot.

I decided to split my platoon using the chopper to divide them. Keeping sure my men continued with suppressive fire I radioed the Captain and was making plans for another medevac when something slammed my leg like a metal fence post. I couldn't move and the pain became unbearable. SSgt. Brown was now in control of 3rd platoon.

The F100 jets were now bombarding the enemy. Each strike rumbled the ground and littered us with dirt. I was being bandaged by Doc Brault who informed me that another medevac was coming in.

SSgt. Lowell W. Brown and Shorty Menendez grabbed my shoulder harness and trouser legs to carry me to the medevac chopper. It felt like we were hitting every hole and boulder on our way to the chopper. Every step sent a wave of searing pain into my knee. It seemed an eternity of time before they lifted me aboard the medevac chopper. Thanks to them I made it out safely.

It took 23 years before I would reunite with SSgt. Brown and Shorty Menendez in Las Vegas, Nevada on July 1993. It was a great experience being with these two men and thank them again for taking me safely to the medevac chopper under intense enemy fire. They risked their life for me.

To all who served with me in Vietnam, You are all heroes. I hope to meet you all again at a reunion.

Eric Schmidt

~~~~~~~~~

John D. Meadows
Columbus, Ohio
Vietnam: December 1969 – April 1970
11-Bravo Rifleman and M79

My memory of that day is limited. I recall we were on a mission at Straight Edge Woods. We arrived prior to our Company's arrival to secure a landing zone. We were in an open field and it was terribly hot and dry. Shorty and I were sitting by the berm waiting for our next move towards the wood line.

When the rest of our Company arrived we were still sitting at the rice paddy dike facing the woods.

Phillip Martin had gone into the woods to pee and made contact with the enemy. We were hit hard by enemy machine gun fire and couldn't move from behind the dike.

When Martin ran from the woods we were fighting to get to cover quickly. Enemy rounds were hitting everywhere around us.

The captain ordered us to do an online assault against the enemy who were well hidden in the woods. We didn't get far before Dale Erdman was killed. I had shot one round from my M79 Grenade Launcher when the spent shell became stuck inside. I was trying to extract the spent shell when I was shot in my hip. I couldn't move my leg or even crawl. They kept shooting at me while I laid there. I could feel the bullets throw the dirt up next to me. Gary Stannish helped me get back safely behind the dike. I remember the overpowering pain in my lower body. All I could see was the blood soaking my jungle fatigues. I remember lying there as Doc Brault bandaged my wound.

A medevac chopper came in and was quickly shot down next to us. I knew the situation would only get worse, just like the pain.

I think the decisions of our Captain that day were horrible. We never should have been ordered to assault an enemy we couldn't see. He could have had us move further away to safe distance until we knew more about the enemy's strength. I did not ever like our Captain.

Gary Stannish helped me get to the arriving second medevac chopper. There were jets dropping bombs as we headed towards the chopper. Gary and the helicopter medic were helping me get into the chopper while enemy rounds continued to strike its hull. I could clearly hear the rounds hit. I remember thinking I was truly going to die in the medevac chopper. It was a great feeling when the chopper lifted off the ground and quickly banked away from the battle area.

I was flown immediately to Tay Ninh Base Camp Field Hospital. It was during my initial triage that they discovered I had been wounded two additional times to my leg.

I don't remember much more except that during the next couple of days Lt. Schmidt was in the hospital bed next to mine. SSgt. Brown, Shorty Menendez and Gary Stannish were able to come visit me before I was flown out of country for emergency surgery.

We were reunited some 35 years later at one of our Company reunions. That was a great day.

John D. Meadows

~~~~~~~~~

This is a letter I, Gary Harding, received from MARY BARGER, sister of Harry Daniel "Danny" Jojola. Daniel was a member of our Company's First Platoon. He was a soldier killed the morning of this battle.

The information is from a member of the 2nd platoon who wrote of his death to her.

-IN LOVING MEMORY OF OUR BROTHER-

On April 7, 1970 our company attempted to assault a u-shaped wooded area from an open field. The woods were called "The Straight Edge Woods", map coordinates # XT179293. The Company was opposed by an unknown number of North Vietnamese Army (NVA) troops.

On this day First Platoon was led by First Lieutenant John E. Hill, who was an Army Ranger. They were to protect the Company's left flank. As they approached the edge of the woods, the point man, SP4 Michael Paulson, was killed. First Lieutenant Hill was also wounded in his leg. Danny attempted to pull Lt. Hill out of the woods but the lieutenant was caught up in some heavy vines. Danny went back to the field to get another soldier to help in the Lt's rescue. While Danny helped untangle the Lt. the enemy opened fire killing both Danny and Lt. Hill.

Second Platoon (my platoon) formed a line and began firing at the suspected enemy position in the wood line.

A dust-off medevac was called in but it was shot down. The medevac pilot was First Lieutenant Douglas G. MacNiel, 159 Medical Detachment. He was killed while attempting a courageous landing to evacuate wounded soldiers. The crew members were all wounded except for the medic.

That night we pulled back away from the woods and set up a night defensive perimeter. We observed the enemy lining up along the wood around midnight. We had no available artillery support available if they decided to attack us. The NVA went off towards Cambodia.

The next morning we returned to retrieve our fallen soldiers.

On that day, April 7, 1970 men of Charlie Company and one U.S. pilot were taken away from us. A memorial service was held at our Tay Ninh base camp a few days later.

This battle is remembered by all of Charlie Company and is often talked about at our reunions.

Gary A. Harding
Littleton, Ohio,
Vietnam, 1969-70,
2nd. Platoon, 3/22nd Infantry Brigade,
25th Infantry Division

~~~~~~~~

1st. Lt. John Cruz
Forward Observer
Nick name was – *FO*
HOME STATE- California

On April 7, 1970, Charlie Company, 3rd Battalion, 22nd Infantry was air lifted into a landing zone adjacent to an area commonly known as the "Straight Edge Woods". Our landings were usually preceded by artillery prep along the tree line of our drop zone. But on this day, we were too close to the Cambodian border so there was no prep preceding our landing. Our company, consisting of 4 line platoons along with a weapons platoon, had operated in this area before and knew it had a history of strong enemy presence.

Usually in an air mobile assault, the infantrymen will vacate a chopper as soon as the chopper hits the ground, then the soldiers immediately make their way to the nearest wood line to get out of an exposed position. This is common practice. The last thing an infantry soldier wants to do is stick around on a *hot* LZ. This was not a hot LZ, but for some reasons our commanding officer, Captain Lawson Pride, kept the company out on the landing zone, a very dangerous tactic. Usually our company would immediately move toward a tree line, in order to be out of the line of enemy contact. At first, I thought Captain Pride was trying to get his bearing but after a while I grew nervous standing out in an exposed area with a very ominous wood line facing us. I wasn't the only one concerned. The CHU Hoi scouts (former Viet Cong who now worked for the U.S. Military) sensed that this was a bad area and a very vulnerable position and immediately started digging a foxhole in this exposed area. This was not a good sign and should have signaled to Captain Pride that his company was exposed and needed to move to a more guarded area. We remained out in the open while the weapons platoon (mortar artillery) set up in an area south of the rest of the company's position.

While we were sitting out on the landing zone, a member of our point squad (our lead element) noticed some movement in the tree line adjacent to the open area. Instead of immediately moving his company into a more secure area and sending a squad to investigate, Captain Pride chose to line up the entire company, shoulder to shoulder, out in the open area for a single-line assault on the tree line. It was a terrible tactic last used during the Civil War. Upon his command, we moved in a single file on an enemy position which was hidden in the tree line.

Who knows what awaited us. We had no clue as to the size and strength of the enemy. No sooner did we begin our assault when the enemy opened fire at us. We were sitting ducks. We returned a heavy volume of fire and eventually made it to the tree line but because of our exposed position several men were wounded and killed during the assault.

Once in the tree line and our positions were finally secured, a medevac was called for the wounded and killed.

Sitting in the tree line, we could see the medevac making its approach toward the open area. Upon making its final approach, the medevac was hit by small arms fire and exploded and crashed. The pilot was killed but the rest of the crew survived. A second medevac was called in and it successfully retrieved the wounded and most of the KIA'S.

Meanwhile elements of Charlie Company came in heavy contact with the enemy along the perimeter of the woods. While investigating a trail, Lt. John Hill, one of the company's platoon leaders, was killed as he tried to rescue one of his casualties. Apparently, Lt. Hill's platoon had come in contact with multiple enemies hidden in bunkers.

We pulled back from the woods and moved further away out in the field where we stayed all night. The next day we returned to the wood line to retrieve other casualties

Lt. John Cruz

~~~~~~~~

SSgt. Lowell Wayne Brown
Infantry Airborne
3rd Platoon Sargent and Platoon Leader, 1969-1970
Occupation, 4th generation Farmer
Hometown- Chuckey, TN

I remember returning to Charlie Company Headquarters at Fire Support Base Washington after recouping from a bad kidney stone.   Our First Sargent said my platoon was sweeping the south edge of Straight Edge Woods in preparation for a company landing the next morning. He said I could join up with my platoon by getting on the next day's air-lift carrying supplies to the Company's landing zone.

When I landed at the platoon's position I immediately joined with them (3rd platoon) and became their platoon Sargent once again.

The next morning of April 7th we waited at the landing zone where the rest of the company was scheduled to arrive.   Lt. Schmidt organized the men along a low berm line parallel to the woods.   When the company arrived Capt. Pride had the company stay in the open area away from the wood line. I was very nervous about staying in the open.   Lt. Schmidt said we should move further away from the main body of the Company along the berm for safety and a better fighting position.

It wasn't but a few minutes later that the crack of an AK47and a M16 rifles rang out from within the woods. I began checking my men to see who may be missing. It was Phillip Martin in the woods.

Lt. Schmidt along with Gary Stannish went to the wood line to find Martin. Martin came running from the woods yelling, *"gooks in the woods, gooks in the woods"*.

Lt. Schmidt, Gary Stannish and Martin all made a fast dash back to the berm safely. It was then that many of the enemy began to fire at our platoon. We could hear explosions at the far end of the Company's position. Automatic machine gun fire was now erupting everywhere along the berm line. At this time I moved my position to the far right of the platoon's line which allowed me and Lt. Schmidt better control over the men.

Captain Pride ordered the Company to form an online assault against the wood line. We questioned the order, but it was given again and we all obeyed.

Walking toward the woods, we confronted the enemy firing heavily at them into a dark jungle. We had only moved forward a few steps when Dale Erdman was hit by automatic gun fire and he fell backward to the ground. Our medic, Doc. Bob Brault and I carried Dale back behind the berm. I held Dale in my arms while Doc. tried to save him but the wound was deadly.

In those same few seconds John Meadows was also badly wounded in his hip. He was unable to return to the berm without help. Gary Stannish was able to reach him and return back to the safety of the platoon.

I will never forget Dale dying in my arms. I'm awed that we all were not killed.

After returning to the berm and the platoon, I low crawled to the Captain's position to suggest he divert incoming air support to my platoon's immediate front. The enemy's weapons fire was heavier there. The Capt. had no idea of the enemy's strength, and he refused.

I was returning back to my platoon's position when I saw Lt. Schmidt fall to the ground and he began cry out in pain as he clutched at his knee. An enemy sniper had found the Lieutenant in his sights.

The whole Company pulled back away from the wood line in the mid-afternoon heat to a more safe distance, further out into the field. There was no further contact with the enemy.

The next morning we returned to the woods edge and saw the carnage of the battle.

This was my last battle in Vietnam with Charlie Company, and as Platoon Sargent for the 3rd Platoon. It was my time to DEROS home, (DEROS - Date Eligible for Return from Overseas). It was a hell of a way to end my service in Vietnam.

I am proud, honored and privileged to have served with these men.

L. Wayne Brown

~~~~~~~~

Lt. Stephen J. Candela, M.D.
Bravo Company, 3/22 Infantry
Second Platoon Leader
Author; 'Veteran of a Foreign War, From Fox
Hole to Physician'.

    The first month I was there, nothing
terrible seemed to happen. Then suddenly,
one of our companies, Charlie Company,
became engaged in a fierce battle in one of
the jungle areas called `The Straight Edge
Woods'. They had landed in a clearing and
did not go immediately into the tree line.
They waited in the field. Their commander
thought he was going to be transported back
to base camp and was upset he had been
deposited in the field. One of his soldiers
who had gone into the woods to relieve
himself, came running out yelling that there
were a lot of enemy soldiers inside the tree
line.

    One platoon leader, a young West
Point lieutenant, went into the tree line with
some of his platoon. The enemy had a well-
established ambush position and already
knew they were there. Essentially, they used

him as bait after killing his point man. He suffered severe wounds from which he later died. A soldier who tried to pull the lieutenant out was also killed.

The company commander had his men attack several times against the fortified position of the enemy. The attacking soldiers were exposed out in the open, taking many casualties. They lost two of the four platoon leaders in Charlie Company that day.

The life span of a lieutenant or a platoon leader in combat wasn't very great. He had to expose himself to a great deal of fire near the heat of action all the time. We lost four of sixteen platoon leaders; dead in my first month in Vietnam. Several others were wounded.

Eventually, gunships were called in along with air strikes and napalm. My unit, Bravo Company, was called in to block the woods on the opposite side (east side). Before this battle, my Company Commander had turned to me and said, "Steve, can you please take the first wave in for me?"

What could I have said? He was my commanding Officer. I said "Yes Sir".

We flew in on helicopters. We arrived at the battle scene, circling above. I could see the artillery explosions followed by air strikes in the landing zone. I was too focused to be frightened and I was fascinated by the fireworks. Our pilots made their landing approaches with Cobra gunships at our sides: firing rockets, mini-guns and machine-guns. At the last minute the Cobras broke off and our door gunners opened up from the sides of their Hueys (UH1 helicopters) with M-60 machine guns: A true ride of the Valkyries.

We stood on the landing skids starting at 300 feet and before touchdown, we jumped from the aircraft, not wanting to be in or near a helicopter that might be hit by a RPG. This was a mutual feeling and an understanding between us grunts and the flyboys. We needed to get out of the dangerous position and they in turn, needed our protection on the ground.

I led my men straight to the tree line. Bullets were whizzing like angry hornets, but I didn't want to allow the enemy to get their heads up before we got there. This was the best time after the suppressive fire to get into an enemy's position. We secured the tree line. There was no significant resistance, for which I was grateful. We then proceeded to dig for a blocking position. Bullets were still flying all around with heavy artillery, mortar and gunship fire was heard sporadically throughout the day and night.

Early the next day we relieved Charlie Company and moved in to clear the enemy bunker complex. The enemy had already gone. We recovered a few VC flags and some equipment. The enemy had left and evacuated most of their dead and wounded. There were sniper bodies hanging in harnesses from the trees where they had been killed or fried by napalm.

One of the previous day's helicopters had been shot down and our company secured it. The pilot had been on his third tour, volunteering to fly this rescue mission. He was a brave man who gave his life for others. The Red Cross emblazoned on his helicopter just made a big target and never meant anything to the communist, just as they usually never took prisoners, claiming it was too difficult to care for them. I was glad it was over.

~~~~~~~~~

PFC Teddy Mike Secrease
Infantry
Charlie Company, 3rd Battalion, 22nd Infantry
25th Infantry Division
1st Platoon - M60 Machine Gun Operator
Vietnam 1969-1970
Hometown: Havre, Montana

I remember when the helicopters came to pick us up we were relieved, as we thought we were going to the rear. We had already been out on a mission for 3-4 days ("we" being Charlie Company). I was especially relieved, as the inseam of my pants had started to give way.

2nd Platoon was in the rice paddy next to a termite mound when they dropped us off. I was carrying a basic load of ammo, about 400 rounds for my M60 machine gun. From our position, we heard a few rounds fired off as one of men from 3rd platoon was in the trees going to the bathroom. We thought the gun fire was from a sniper.

Capt. Pride ordered us to get on line. We had 3rd Platoon to our right. They told us to attack the wood line. As soon as we stepped out from behind the berm, everything just exploded. Bullets were flying everywhere. After taking about 2 steps, everyone just dropped to the ground, returned fire, and started crawling back to the berm. They continued firing at us from the woods directly in front of us.

Capt. Pride told Lt. Hill to take a squad and try to flank the enemy's position. So we proceeded to the left, away from the termite mound and across the rice paddy to the wood line. 3rd platoon was still getting hit pretty hard from the woods and there were still a lot of stray (so we thought at the time) bullets flying past us. Mike Paulson was the point man for our squad and was the first to find a trailhead opening to enter into the woods. I don't remember who was walking slack (the last man in line). Lt. Hill was the third man, followed by Russ Tipton, RTO (radio transmission operator). Then it was me and my assistant gunner Jerry. Just as Lt. Hill got to the edge of the woods, all hell broke loose. Paulson was wounded and Lt. Hill was trying to get ahold of his leg to pull him back and he was wounded himself. Sgt.

Jojola moved forward and grabbed the Lt.'s legs to pull him back but couldn't move him, so he called for help. My assistant gunner Jerry moved forward to help Lt. Hill at which time the enemy emptied a whole clip (30 bullets) into Lt. Hill which killed him, killed Sgt. Jojola and wounded Jerry. Tipton was returning fire and calling for help on the radio at the same time. I was on the ground returning cover fire during this time. I was down to 300-400 rounds, between my ammo and what Jerry had been carrying. Somebody (I don't remember who) grabbed Jerry's arm and pulled him back while Tipton and I continued to lay down covering fire.

Once they made it back to the berm, Tipton called back for support to help get us out from where we were pinned down, there were just the 2 of us left alive by this time. I remember Russ Tipton turning to me and saying "We're on our own, they're not sending anybody." I was down to about 200 rounds. They fired an RPG that bounced towards us. I didn't know what it was at the time, just saw a puff of dust and felt it bounce between the bipod legs of the gun, then saw it bounce against a tree and explode about a hundred yards away.

I was trying to get Tipton to make a run for it while I covered him with the last 200 rounds, but he said no, he wanted us to run together. I looked back towards the company and saw a lone figure running towards us, covered in M60 ammo. I finished emptying the M60 to give him cover until he got to us. It was Manning. He had been my previous assistant gunner who had gone on to carrying a gun himself. I asked him "What the hell are you doing?" and he said "I heard the company commander say you were on your own, and figured you might need some more ammo." With the extra ammo, we set up and reloaded the machine gun. We then stood up firing, walking backwards toward the berm (me, Tipton, and Manning). When getting up to start back, the final stitches of my pants inseam gave way, so now I was wearing a skirt instead of trousers. Halfway back the gun double fed and a round cooked off in the chamber, ruining the gun. We spun and ran for the berm, my pants flapping around my legs as I ran. I still say the reason they didn't hit us is because the enemy was laughing too hard at the sight of my bare white ass running through the rice paddy!

We got there just as the medevac helicopter was shot down. We regrouped along the berm and the rest of the 1st platoon rejoined us. Word came down that a re-supply of food and ammo was coming in on another medevac. I was very relieved when the re-supply showed up to get a new pair of pants, almost as important as the ammo! They told us that once the re-supply was there, we had to go back for the bodies (Mike Paulson, Danny Jojola, and Lt. Hill). I didn't know what to do for a weapon since mine was ruined. I heard that Gary Harding had the M60 from the downed chopper. I was able to move down the line and talk him out of it.

Once we were re-supplied with ammo, we moved back to where we had just retreated, at the edge of the woods. Almost immediately they started firing RPG's and small arms fire at us. The air felt as heavy as lead to breathe. As the bullets were flying by us, we tried to move forward attempting to get the bodies out. One of our new sergeants was in a position slightly behind and to my right. He was hit by one of the RPG's, which took off the top of his shoulder. Thank God we were too close for the RPG to have armed itself. They were ripping us up. My gun jammed. I had to take it apart and disassemble the gas cylinder operating plug to clear it and put it back together, all the while under fire. We had one or two more guys wounded and finally received an order to pull back. They pulled out our wounded while we laid down cover fire and then the rest of the platoon headed back. We were unable to recover any of our killed soldiers. Word came down that an airstrike was inbound.

After the airstrikes and the medevac came and went, we got word that we had to go back in to retrieve the bodies of our comrades. We moved forward again, this time we were able to recover Hill and Jojola. The firing intensity coming at us had not let up at all, so we were unable to get to Paulsen. By this time, everyone was running low on ammo again. They told us to move further out into the rice paddy field to dig in and set up NDP's (Night Defensive Positions), as they wouldn't be able to re-supply us again that day or pick up the dead. Everyone was critically low on ammo. As it got dark, the Starlight Scope operators told us we had enemy coming out of the wood line toward us. The company was calling for any kind of air or artillery support and was told there was none available. One of the platoon sergeants said to "Fix bayonets" as they'd counted over 100 enemy soldiers coming out of the woods towards us.

The enemy got halfway to where we were, and then they turned and walked towards Cambodia. We stayed where we were, apprehensive all night. I kept looking at the poncho covered bodies of my friends and wondered who would cover us up. I don't think anybody slept. The next morning the choppers came in for us and we returned to our base camp.

After that battle, my time in Vietnam was never the same. I had lost all hope of making it out of Vietnam alive. I had the mindset to take out as many of the enemy as I could. We had some other missions in April after the battle at Straight Edge Woods. We then did a month in a major offensive into Cambodia in May.

I remained in a state of mental detachment for the last 2 ½ months that I remained in Vietnam. All of my memories of my time in Vietnam after the battle at Straight Edge Woods have been a blur. I've continued to have vivid nightmares all of these years after this battle.

I am proud to have served with all of these honorable men in C/3/22.

Teddy (Mike) Secrease

Mike Secrease with his M60 machine gun

First Lieutenant Doug MacNiel-Dust-off 163

Killed In Action 07 April, 1970

32 Years Old, Single, Born May 30, 1937
From: Queens Village, New York.
Military service was 3 years.
His tour of duty began On June 04, 1968

Vietnam Memorial Panel 12W - Line104

"NO MAN HAS GREATER LOVE THAN TO LAY
DOWN HIS OWN LIFE FOR HIS BROTHERS."

Mac's Last Flight

By a Crewmember of that day (Name
Respectfully Withheld)

"Dust-off 163, this is Tay Ninh Dust-off, over".
The Tay Ninh standby crew was busy that day. Two operations were in progress southwest of Tay Ninh, and the 22nd Infantry Regiment of the 25th Infantry Division ran into two North Vietnamese Regiments in the Straight Edge Woods and Renegade Woods near the Angel's Wing.

Dust-off 163, 1LT Doug MacNeil was the aircraft commander. The medic was PFC Ed Iannuccilli, the crew chief was SP/4 Mark McKinna, and WO1 Ted Howard was the co-pilot. We had evacuated some wounded from the operations northeast of Tay Ninh to the 45th MAST Hospital at Tay Ninh base camp. We were refueling at the airstrip when we received the request for an urgent evac for US wounded in the Straight Edge Woods. We stopped the refueling and proceeded to the area. When we arrived, the pickup site was under intense enemy fire. As the gunships engaged the enemy, Dust-off 163 circled a few miles to the west, on the edge of the Cambodian border, monitoring the battle on the radio.

After circling for several minutes (precious minutes to the patient), Dust-off 163 made the decision to make the pickup. Doug flew low-level and fast towards the site, and announced over the radio to the gunships and the ground troops that he was approaching from the west. After spotting the pickup point, he decelerated with a side flare. As he was keeping eye contact with the landing point, the enemy opened fire from the woods with a heavy machine gun and small arms fire. The aircraft took many hits and sustained severe damage.

The initial burst of fire hit the engine and the crew. The aircraft, still in a side-flare, crashed from about 15 feet above the ground. Lt. MacNeil was killed instantly with several bullets to his chest. WO1 Howard was hit in both legs and his feet were knocked from the controls. SP/4 McKinna was hit seconds later in the hip and leg. The medic was unhurt by enemy fire or by the crash. The medic and crew chief were able to exit the aircraft immediately. The co-pilot escaped later with the help of the medic and ground troops who had crawled back into the burning aircraft and broke out the front window. They were not able to recover Doug MacNeil from the aircraft which was now fully consumed by fire.

The gunships were reinforced and were able to intensify the fire on the enemy forces. The crew was rescued by another aircraft in the area, and was flown back to the 45th Hospital in Tay Ninh. The urgent patient they had been called to rescue died of his wounds.

~~~~~~~~~~

Stephen Shorty Menendez

Vietnam 1969 – 1970
Charlie Company, 3rd Battalion,
22nd Infantry Brigade, 25th Infantry Division
3rd Platoon (third herd)
Rifleman, Tunnel Rat
U.S. Army, 1969-1975
Now Residing in Chuckey, Tennessee
Author; *"Journey into Darkness, a Tunnel Rats Story "*
and *"Battle at Straight Edge Woods "*

My letter of remembrance is this book. I can say that it was a remarkable experience and honor to serve with these men. One of my greatest joys is the friendship we still have.

When I decided to write about this Battle at Straight Edge Woods, it really never occurred to me the deep feelings of loss which I and each man of Charlie Company have tried to overcome. This record of that battle and memories of the soldiers who fought that day have shown how horrible battle is. *All* were heroes on that day.

We can look at each other when we meet and know we all did our best. I recollect the battle and these men like it happened just yesterday.

I believe this battle to have been one of our most tormenting losses. I remember how after these battles many of us would drift away in a confused depressed somber. Some were lucky to have a close platoon unity to console one another. It seems we still have that connection after 40+ years. Sometimes we became numb to the loss of a fellow soldier after a battle. We hadn't enough life experience to handle or understand it all. We carry the losses and memories in our mind and hearts.

We would do it all again for our country.

It was the camaraderie between us that passed on respect from one soldier to another. We were not all meant to be leaders. I don't believe we had a fellow soldier killed or wounded that we didn't weep for after a battle.

We still wonder why we were lucky not to be killed ourselves. I remember the respect I felt for a later Company Captain of Charlie Company, (James K. Skiles) who called our unit together to bring remembrance and prayer for one soldier who was killed during an ambush. This Captain *did* know his soldiers by their given name.

I hope history will be accurate to tell everyone that we did our best as young soldiers.

Many times I had to stop writing this book and letters of recall from my brothers of Charlie Company. It was hard for me to do mentally. Many of the guys said they just didn't want to bring up all those dreadful memories again. But all these men did encourage me to write of this battle. I knew we must remember our brothers who died that day. They *must* be remembered. Let us also remember those in this battle that were wounded. They forever carry the physical scars of this battle. We will all carry mental scars of that day forever.

I know there were many other devastating battles in Vietnam that some say were historical in nature. I found out one important thing about all battles, *someone dies*.

History is made from every battle fought in the name of freedom. Let us remember this piece of history and those who fought gallantly in the battle.

"I will always remember these men."

KIA'S of April 7, 1970

Dale A. Erdman
John E. Hill
Harry D. Jojola
Michael Paulsen
Doug MacNiel, medevac helicopter pilot

Made in the USA
Monee, IL
18 January 2022